City Girl, Country Boy

Fiona Kenshole

T0347100

Name _____

Age _____

Class _____

OXFORD
UNIVERSITY PRESS

OXFORD
UNIVERSITY PRESS

Great Clarendon Street, Oxford OX2 6DP

Oxford University Press is a department of the University of Oxford.
It furthers the University's objective of excellence in research, scholarship,
and education by publishing worldwide in

Oxford New York

Auckland Bangkok Buenos Aires Cape Town Chennai
Dar es Salaam Delhi Hong Kong Istanbul Karachi Kolkata
Kuala Lumpur Madrid Melbourne Mexico City Mumbai
Nairobi São Paulo Shanghai Taipei Tokyo Toronto

OXFORD and OXFORD ENGLISH are registered trade marks of
Oxford University Press in the UK and in certain other countries

© Oxford University Press 2005

The moral rights of the author have been asserted

Database right Oxford University Press (maker)

First published 2005

2023

22

ISBN-13: 978 0 19 440112 8
ISBN-10: 0 19 440112 x

Printed in China

Illustrations by: Geo Parkin
With thanks to Sally Spray for her contribution to this series

📖 Using the book

1 Begin by looking at the first story page (page 2). Look at the picture and ask questions about it. Then read the story text under the picture with your students. **Use section 1 of the CD for this if possible.**

2 Teach and check the understanding of any new vocabulary. Note that some of the words are in the **Picture Dictionary** at the back of the book.

3 Now look at the activities on the right-hand page. Show the example to the students and instruct them to complete the activities. This may be done individually, in pairs, or as a class.

4 Do the same for the remaining pages of the book.

5 Retell the whole story more quickly, reinforcing the new vocabulary. **Section 2 of the CD can help with this.**

6 **If possible, listen to the expanded story (section 3 of the CD). The students should follow in their books.**

7 When the book is finished, use the **Picture Dictionary** to check that students understand and remember new vocabulary. **Section 4 of the CD can help with this.**

💿 Using the CD

The CD contains four sections.

1 The story told slowly, with pauses. Use this during the first reading. It may also be used for "Listen and repeat" activities at any point.

2 The story told at normal speed. This should be used once the students have read the book for the first time.

3 The expanded story. The story is told in a longer version. This will help the students understand English when it is spoken faster, as they will now know the story and the vocabulary.

4 Vocabulary. Each word in the **Picture Dictionary** is spoken and then used in a simple sentence.

Tim lives on a farm in the country. He is on his way to visit his cousin Anna in the city. Anna and her mother are waiting to meet him at the train station.

This is Tim's first visit to the big city. He is very excited.

Check ☑ true or false.

		True	False
❶	Tim lives in the country.	☑	☐
❷	Tim is going to visit his cousin.	☐	☐
❸	Tim is going to the city.	☐	☐
❹	Tim is on the train.	☐	☐
❺	Anna is Tim's cousin.	☐	☐
❻	Tim often goes to the city.	☐	☐
❼	Tim's uncle is waiting for him.	☐	☐
❽	Tim is very excited.	☐	☐
❾	He can see an airplane through the train window.	☐	☐
❿	He can see tall buildings.	☐	☐

Tim is in Anna's apartment, at the top of a
tall building.

"Wow! Look at all those buildings. Look
at all those cars and buses. The people are
so small. They look like ants from up here.
You're really lucky, Anna."

1 **What does Tim see on page 4?**

Tim sees ___buildings___, _____,

_____, and _____.

2 **What other things do you see here?**

I see _____, _____,

_____, and _____.

It is midnight. Anna is asleep. Tim is in a
big, comfortable bed, but he cannot sleep.
There are a lot of lights. He can hear a fire
engine, some police cars, a big motorcycle,
and there is a helicopter flying overhead.

The city is really noisy at night.

Answer the questions.

1 What time is it?

It is midnight.

2 Is Anna in bed?

_____

3 Is Anna sleeping?

_____

4 Is Tim in bed?

_____

5 Is Tim sleeping?

_____

6 Why can't he sleep?

_____

7 What can he hear?

_____

8 Can you sleep well in the city?

_____

The next morning, they are on the
subway. Anna is taking Tim to a roller
disco. There are so many people on the
subway. It's dirty and crowded, and they
cannot sit down. Tim is getting very tired.

How did they get to the roller disco? Complete.

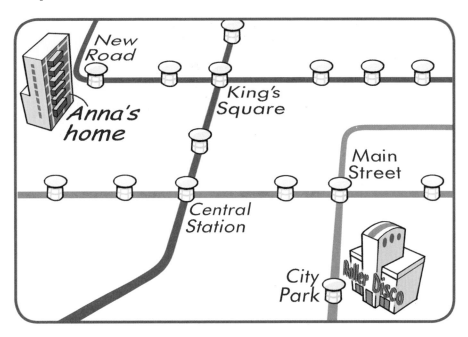

They took the ___red___ line from

New Road to _____ station. Then

they changed to the _____ line and took

the train to _____. Then they

took the _____ line and changed at

_____ station, and then they took the

_____ line and got off at _____

station.

"Isn't it great?" says Anna. "I come here every week with my friends. Isn't the music wonderful?"

"The music is too loud!" says Tim.

"Put on your rollerblades and let's go!"

"But everyone is skating so fast! I can't skate that fast!"

Look at the pictures. Complete using the words in the box.

bed big cake city coffee cold hot
noisy soft sweater sweet weather

❶ The __weather__ is too __cold__.

❷ The _____ is too _____.

❸ The _____ is too _____.

❹ The _____ is too _____.

❺ The _____ is too _____.

❻ The _____ is too _____.

"Did you enjoy the roller disco?" asks Anna.

"It was OK."

"I'm so thirsty. I really need this drink."

"What's it called?" asks Tim.

"It's a Timbuktu Twist."

"It looks great! How do you drink it?"

How do you make a Timbuktu Twist?
Check ✓ seven things.

✓ You need a tall glass and a straw.

☐ Open your pencil case.

☐ Buy some pizza at the supermarket.

☐ Pour orange juice into the glass.

☐ Cut an apple into small squares.

☐ Take your dog for a walk.

☐ Put the apple squares in with the juice.

☐ Call your friend on the telephone.

☐ Add some ice cream.

☐ Add some nice green mint sauce.

☐ Cut up a lemon and put it on top.

☐ Sit down on a comfortable chair.

Tim and Anna are walking home. They have to cross a big road. The light changes, so they start to walk across the road. Suddenly, a big yellow taxi turns the corner. It is going too fast and it almost hits them.

Rearrange the words.

1 Anna's Tim cousin is

  Tim is Anna's cousin.

2 the went they roller to together disco

_____

3 are Anna and Tim home walking

_____

4 the is green light

_____

5 fast taxi going too is the

_____

6 the and in Tim are road Anna

_____

7 children the hits almost taxi the

_____

8 afraid Anna Tim are and

_____

"It's time for me to go back to the country," says Tim.

"I hope you had a good time," says Anna.

"It was OK, thank you. It's your turn to visit me in the country."

"OK. That sounds wonderful."

Put the sentences in order.
Number them 1–12.

☐ They took the subway.

☐ They went to Anna's apartment.

☐ They walked home.

☐ They went to the roller disco.

☐ Tim asked Anna to visit him on the farm.

1 Tim went to the city by train.

☐ They had a drink called a Timbuktu Twist.

☐ Tim saw a beautiful view of the city.

☐ A taxi almost hit them.

☐ Anna and her mother met him at the station.

☐ Tim went back to the country.

☐ Tim could not sleep.

Anna is visiting Tim in the country for the first time. Tim's father is driving them home from the train station. Anna is happy. She loves animals, so she wants to see the farm.

"Welcome to the country!" says Tim.

Rewrite the sentences correcting the underlined words.

❶ Anna is <u>visit</u> Tim.

Anna is visiting Tim.

❷ Tim's father is <u>drive</u> the truck.

_____

❸ They are <u>sit</u> on the back of the truck.

_____

❹ Anna <u>are</u> happy.

_____

❺ Tim <u>live</u> on a farm.

_____

❻ They are <u>go</u> to the farm.

_____

❼ Anna <u>love</u> animals.

_____

❽ Tim <u>have</u> many animals on the farm.

_____

"It's so beautiful here!" says Anna. "Look at all the animals."

"Yes, we have cows, sheep, chickens, ducks, and a pony called Star."

"You're so lucky, Tim!"

1 Connect.

chicken •
cow •
dog •
duck •
farm •
goat •
horse •
mouse •
owl •
pony •
sheep •

2 Use the words in Activity 1 to complete the crossword.

It is nine o'clock. Everyone except Anna is asleep. Her eyes are wide open but she can't see anything because it is so dark. She can hear the farm animals. There's an owl at the window. It makes a sound like a ghost. Anna is afraid.

Circle the words and make a sentence.

Anna	eats	off	the	big	town
Tim	comes	from	an	small	city

1 _Anna comes from the big city._

It	is	not	o'clock	to	night
They	am	nine	seventy	at	morning

2 _____

Tim	is	afraid	of	a	dog
Anna	are	cold	to	an	owl

3 _____

Anna	is	not	in	the	dark
It	cannot	see	on	a	house

4 _____

The	owl	today	is	a	apple
A	cat	sounds	like	an	ghost

5 _____

The next day, Tim and Anna are outside. It's a beautiful day. Tim shows Anna how to ride his pony. Tim rides very well. It looks easy. Now it's Anna's turn, but it's not that easy.

"Hold on tight, Anna," says Tim.

1 Rewrite and punctuate the story.

the next morning tim and anna are at school
it's a rainy day tim shows anna how to use a
computer tim types very quickly it looks easy
now it's anna's turn but it's not that easy you
are doing very well anna says tim

The next morning, Tim and Anna

are at school.

2 Write another story about Tim and Anna.

Later Tim takes Anna out in a boat. They
are both fishing.

"Are you sure there are fish in this
pond?" asks Anna. "I'm getting bored."

"Bored? Just wait a few more minutes."

Make sentences about Anna and Tim.
Use the words in the water.

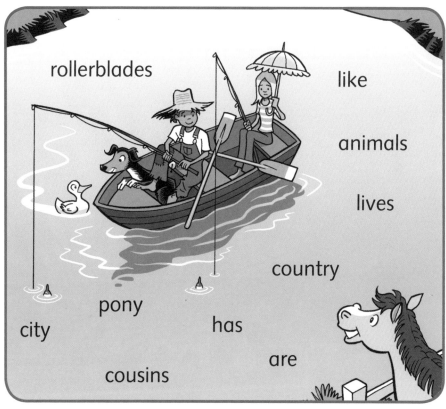

Anna _lives in the city._

Anna _____

Tim _____

Tim _____

Anna and Tim _____

Anna and Tim _____

"Wow, you caught a big one," says Tim.
But Anna falls into the water.

"Help!" she says. "I can't swim."

"It's OK! The water isn't deep," says
Tim. "Just stand up."

Where did Tim and Anna go? Connect.

Tim took Anna to see the farm. They walked from the farmhouse to the chicken house, then down the road to the barn. They got on the pony and went through the forest to see the sheep. Then they walked over a bridge into a field with cows in it and they had a picnic under an apple tree. Then they crossed the river and went down to the pond. They took a boat to the island.

Back at home in the city, Anna calls Tim.

"Did you have a good time?" asks Tim.

"It was OK, but I prefer the city."

"You prefer the city and I prefer the country," says Tim.

"See you, Tim"

"OK. Goodbye."

Complete.

Tim _____ in the country.

He goes to visit his _____

Anna in the _____. Tim sees many

_____, people, and cars in _____

city. They go to the roller _____ and a

restaurant. Tim doesn't _____ the city

_____ much.

Anna _____ to visit Tim in

the _____. She sees many

_____ there. They _____ a pony

and they go _____ . Anna catches a

_____, and falls into the _____.

Anna _____ like the country very

_____. She _____ the city.

Picture Dictionary

boat

fire engine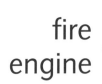

bridge

fish

chicken

goat

cow

helicopter

duck

horse

island

rollerblades

light

sheep

owl

subway

pony

swim

road

Dolphin Readers

Dolphin Readers are available at five levels, from Starter to 4.

The Dolphins series covers four major themes:

Grammar, Living Together, The World Around Us, Science and Nature.

For each theme, there are two titles at every level.

Activity Books are available for all Dolphins.

All Dolphins are available on audio CD.
(2 TITLES ON EACH CD ◯ SEE TABLE BELOW)

Teacher's Notes are available at **www.oup.com/elt/dolphins**

	Grammar	Living Together	The World Around Us	Science and Nature
Starter	• Silly Squirrel • Monkeying Around	• My Family • A Day with Baby	• Doctor, Doctor • Moving House	• A Game of Shapes • Baby Animals
Level 1	• Meet Molly • Where Is It?	• Little Helpers • Jack the Hero	• On Safari • Lost Kitten	• Number Magic • How's the Weather?
Level 2	• Double Trouble • Super Sam	• Candy for Breakfast • Lost!	• A Visit to the City • Matt's Mistake	• Numbers, Numbers Everywhere • Circles and Squares
Level 3	• Students in Space • What Did You Do Yesterday?	• New Girl in School • Uncle Jerry's Great Idea	• Just Like Mine • Wonderful Wild Animals	• Things That Fly • Let's Go to the Rainforest
Level 4	• The Tough Task • Yesterday, Today, and Tomorrow	• We Won the Cup • Up and Down	• Where People Live • City Girl, Country Boy	• In the Ocean • Go, Gorillas, Go